Ebay Excellence

Making Easy Money The Ebay Way

Brad Jones

CONTENTS

INTRODUCTION

Surely you've heard of Ebay? It has been one of the number one ways to make money online since it was introduced to us back in 1995. With buyers and sellers around the globe, the possibilities are practically endless!

Whether you are looking to de-clutter your home or start a full on business from your living room there is great opportunities for you with Ebay. It can serve as a way around having that yard sale you've been dreading or it could replace your day job with some time and diligence.

The reason Ebay is so great is because anyone can set up an account and start selling right from their home with no upfront costs! All you need is some stuff to sell! (And common, we all have stuff around the house we don't need – but somebody might need it and they are likely searching for it on Ebay!)

If you have always wanted to start your own business, work at your own pace, on your own time, then Ebay could be the best way to break the ice. With how simple it is to get started, anyone can do it and anyone who with the right motivation can make quite a bit of money as well.

People all over the world have broken free of the 9-5 routine to sell items in their Ebay store full time and they are all making a reasonable living too.

So why couldn't you be next?

This e-book will help you understand what is needed to start a successful business on Ebay. We will go through all the steps from opening an account, linking PayPal, listing items and even how to promote your business!

HOW DOES EBAY WORK AND CAN I MAKE A LIVING WITH IT?

Is Ebay really a lucrative career path to consider? Of course it is. Since the mid 90's people have been selling items on Ebay and making a killing doing so. Ebay was one of the first places on the internet that you could buy and sell items and to this day it is one of the best opportunities to start an online business

Simply put, Ebay is an auction site. You list items with a minimum bid, people who are interested in this item fight it out until the last minute. The person with the top bid is awarded the item and the seller ships it out. This is the perfect online garage sale, where you can find all sorts of items, rare, common, useful and bizarre at sometimes great and sometimes outrageous prices.

So the answer to your question? Yes, you can make excellent money selling on Ebay with the right inventory and great customer services skills.

You don't have to be super business savvy to create an online store with Ebay and start making money. Once you get started, you won't want to stop! It's a great chance to break out of that day to day routine, make some extra money and do something you can really enjoy! If you are serious about it, you can turn it into a career with time, patience and a little effort.

There is almost no start-up costs (other than any merchandise you don't already own) which makes it one of the easiest and least expensive ways to start a business.

If all this sounds appealing to you, then it's time to get started!

The first thing you need in order to start a business on Ebay is to create a couple of essential accounts: your Ebay account and a PayPal account.

Your Ebay account will be for listing and selling your items and making purchases. Before you sign up with Ebay however, it is recommended that you sign up with PayPal.

PayPal is actually owned by Ebay and is used to handle credit card transactions over the internet. It is the safest, most secure form of making and receiving payments over the web.

Setting up a PayPal Account

Setting up your PayPal account is simple. All you need to register is an e-mail address and a bank debit card or credit card.

The sign up form for PayPal is quick and easy to fill out and all you need is basic information. Name, address, telephone, etc. Once you confirm your e-mail address all you need to do is add your card information and you're ready to go!

(The card is only there for a form of backup payment for instances when your PayPal balance is less than a purchase you are making. All fees associated with PayPal are on the merchants' end of the transaction – meaning when you make a sale, PayPal will take a small percentage, but they charge you nothing when making a purchase.)

Creating an Ebay Account

In order to sell on Ebay you must register an account and confirm your e-mail address. The sign-up form for Ebay is just as easy to fill out as the PayPal form. Just fill out some basic information about yourself, pick a user ID and create a password. Once you do that, confirming your e-mail only takes a couple of seconds.

Once you have set up your account you will be redirected to a welcome page. From there you should see a link that says "Start Selling". Click on this link and you will be prompted to register to sell where you will login using the username and password you just created.

Once you are logged in you will have a chance to review all your information. Check over your address and other personal information. Then you will need to verify your phone number, which can be done by either an automated call or text that sends you a pin.

(Quick tip – if you do not want your home address to be on your items return address, then consider opening up a P.O. Box for this purpose!)

The last thing you will want to do is add your PayPal account and set this to be where any seller fees are taken from. (Of course, Ebay has to make their money somewhere. They do this by charging a small percentage for listing, from the final selling price and for small things that help you grow your business.)

Actions to take:

- Set up a PayPal account with a confirmed e-mail and debit or credit card.

- Set up your Ebay account and confirm your e-mail, phone and address.

LISTING YOUR ITEMS: WHAT TO SELL AND HOW TO SELL IT!

What Should I Sell?

This has to be one of the most commonly asked question by anyone looking to start a business on Ebay. If you ask many successful Ebay sellers they will most likely tell you the same thing – start off selling your own stuff!

Going through your house and collecting up a laundry baskets worth of items that you no longer use or need is a great way to start. This will give you a chance to get your feet wet, see how the selling process works first hand and decide if this is something you really want to stick with long term.

There are a couple of great bonuses to starting with items you already own:

- No initial cost for inventory (if it doesn't sell the first time, you haven't lost anything!).

- You know the item well, so it will be easy to describe.

- You're learning the ropes of Ebay while decluttering your home!

Start Tracking Your Business

Once you have created your account and listed your first few items, it is time to start looking at this from a business point of view. You should create logs of some sort, whether in a notebook with pen and paper or on the computer in a word document or spreadsheet.

You should have logs for the following:

- Which items are currently listed?

- Which items have sold?

- What was the final selling price?

- How much did Ebay and PayPal take out?

- How much were shipping costs for each item?

The purpose of all of these logs is to keep track of what is selling, what is not as well as what is profitable and what is not.

For example, you might have sold some old designer jeans for a great price and once you took out shipping costs and fees you still have a decent amount left over. This could go in your log as an item you should consider selling again.

On the other hand, you may end up selling a set of 5 DVDs for a decent price but when you went to ship them out found the shipping costs were over half of your final selling price for the DVDs. This means you could either try starting the auction at a higher "Buy It Now" price or just scrap the idea of selling used DVDs all together.

Remember, this is why you start with items out of your own home. You will be less likely to take a real loss on any of the items you sell because you didn't go out and buy them to be sold.

Once you have sold a handful of items and made a little profit, you can look these lists over and start deciding what you might want to sell in the future. After all, you will run out of things to declutter your home eventually and if you want to keep selling, you will need to keep stocking inventory.

By keeping accurate logs of all the items that sell and what prices they sell for will help you with a couple of things: deciding what to sell and deciding what your top budget is for any purchases you make for resale.

That last part is super important because if you spend too much on an item you intend to resell, you may not end up making a profit. Just because you paid X amount for it, does not mean it will automatically sell for that price at auction, it could be below or above that amount.

For some items, this is worth putting a "Buy It Now" option on the listing. This will guarantee you get at least that set amount for the item – but it may not sell right away either. This shouldn't worry you too much, you can relist the item as many times as you may need until it sells.

Until you are sure you are ready to start making more of an investment into this business it is a good idea to stick to items that you already own. After you've been bit by the sellers bug though, you will not want to stop – and that's great! – But you need to keep up with your inventory.

We will touch more on this in a later chapter.

Actions to take:

- Go around your home and fill a box or laundry basket with a few items you no longer need or want to start your inventory at no cost.

- Once you list your items, keep logs to keep track of sales, fees and to help make decisions about buying more inventory later on.

THE SECRETS TO A GREAT LISTING ON EBAY

How to Price Items

When you first start selling, you may not have a clue what to price your old house-hold items at. The best way to decide is to search for the same or similar items that are already listed on Ebay and see what they are going for.

In some cases you should simply start the auction with the $0.99 that Ebay automatically sets up. This is great for relatively small, inexpensive items that will not cost much or anything to ship.

Other items though are far too valuable to let go for a potentially far under retail price. This is why researching your items is so important! You want to price your items just under what other sellers are offering in order to draw in business. On the other hand, you don't want to sell at rock bottom prices or it will take ages to generate a decent income!

Title, Description and Photographs

Coming up with a title is relatively easy – simply name your item as specifically as you can. For example, if you are selling a set of fine china, don't simply put: "China Dish Set". Try something a little more specific like "60 Pieces, Setting for 12, Wedgwood "Devon Cottage" China Dish Set".

Yes, this is a long title, but it gives the buyer exactly what they are looking at prior to clicking on your item. This will draw attention to people who really know how to spot a good deal when they see it!

Perhaps the most important thing though, is to have a clear photograph that you have taken yourself of this item. If you use a stock image, you are less likely to sell or get top dollar for your items. People know that using Ebay they will be buying second hand a lot of the time and they want to know the item is in the best condition possible! They cannot possibly believe that your item is good as new if they have not seen it for their own eyes!

It is recommended that you take a picture with a camera that can provide you with great quality. It doesn't need to be a professional camera to start off with, but do not think your cell phone camera is good enough!

You should also try to make sure that the picture has a solid colored background (preferably white, but any color that will allow the item to stand out will work). This gives you the best chance to show off your item to all the potential buyers.

The last big part of listing your item is to write up a short description. Is your product new, like new, gently used? Stating the condition and having a picture of your item to prove that condition is a great selling point for many people.

Describe in detail exactly what is expected to be in the package when it ships out. This will help you avoid any confusion later on that may lead to returns and bad feedback.

Just as important as carefully choosing your description and title is making sure that you proofread everything before putting the listing up! Make sure that everything is spelled properly and that there are no obvious grammar mistakes.

It may seem obvious to some, but many first time sellers make simple mistakes like this and it will cost them sales. Having everything written properly shows that you took your time to make sure everything is correct and it will look that much more professional.

Strategies for Generating Great Sales

There are many different strategies you can use when you are trying to generate more sales from your Ebay store. Above we mentioned the most simple strategy and one that you should use on EVERY ITEM

YOU LIST – researching the item and sell just below the competitions prices. (As long as this is feasible for your item – some people sell in mass amounts for rock bottom prices, if you have multiple of one item, this is a decent strategy to consider but on a single item rock bottom prices will usually cost you money in the long run.)

Free Shipping and Handling

Consider offering free shipping and handling if you know the order will not cost much to ship. Some things, for example, trading cards, are quite light and since you ship by weight, they will probably cost little to nothing to ship. If you can offer free shipping and handling on an item it will entice buyers to choose your item over the same one elsewhere.

After all, if the item is a little less expensive from another seller it might look great – but when they realize that the other person charges for shipping and you don't, guess what, they will pay the extra $5 for the item rather than an extra $10 for shipping!

Use Keywords Properly

In the same way that keywords can help a website or blogger increase traffic to their website, you can increase traffic to your listings. By using precise keywords that people generally use to search the item you are selling you are highly increasing the chances of your item being brought up in a Google or Bing search.

This will also help your item be found more easily in the Ebay search. Either way a person who searches an item is usually looking to purchase so making your item as visible on the web as possible is a great advantage you may have over your competitors.

Use HTML Product Templates

If you are going to list your item with the intention of building your seller account into a business or store, then you should consider using a Product template. These use HTML to bring a more professional and sleek look to your product page.

When you use plain text in your Ebay store people may not take you as seriously as the seller that put just a little more time and effort into their pages. You don't have to be gifted with web designing and HTML in order to do this, there are tons of great, professionally designed templates that you can use.

Relisting Items

This option is great for a few different reasons. If you find that a particular item sells really well then you may want to list it again. Or maybe you have an item that didn't sell last week and you want to give it another go? Either way, Ebay makes this a breeze for sellers.

Since you have already listed the item before you can simply relist an old listing and all your old information will be prefilled out for you. This makes the listing process much less of a hassle, so when you find trends it may be a good idea to stock up and sell more than one of that item.

Grouping Orders

If you have multiple items for sale then one great option is grouping and offering a discount for doing so. For example if you are selling a pair of designer jeans, a belt and a hat all by the same designer – give them the idea to buy them all with a discount on shipping or a discount on the whole package deal. This is a great way to boost your sales if you have a lot of items that could easily sell as a whole order.

Actions to take:

- Create a great listing: use a specific title, a detailed description and a clear photograph that shows your item at its best. Don't forget to spellcheck!

- Use one or more of the strategies above to boost the number of sales. (Using multiple techniques like relisting, grouping and using keywords will give you the best results in generating bigger revenues.)

THE INS AND OUTS OF SHIPPING AND HANDLING

You should consider shipping costs when listing your items, but that should not be a big worry. Most items are relatively easy to ship and don't cost much. If you listed your item with a free shipping option then you are choosing to cover shipping costs yourself. For some items this is a feasible move to make, after all, it will put you ahead of some of the competition.

When you are considering whether or not to charge for shipping, take a few different things into consideration:

- Is your item heavy? (Most packages are priced by weight at the post office, FedEx or UPS.)

- Do you have packaging? (Boxes, tape, bubble wrap or packing peanuts.)

Preparing for Shipping Costs

When you are in the stage of considering shipping costs for any given item, the best thing you can do is try to calculate the shipping costs. To do this there are options on Ebay like a series of tables that will give you an estimate based on the type of item or the weight of the item. To be most accurate though, often times the best thing you can do is package it up and weigh it!

When you are just starting out it may be worth it to make the trip to the post office after packaging up your item (without sealing it) to weigh it and get a postage estimate. Though once you become a serious seller, this will not be as cost-effective as spending a little money investing in a postage scale.

A postage scale can be bought at almost any retail store like Wal-Mart and usually don't cost more than $25-$30. This means in the long run you will be saving a lot of money in gas and time for trips to the post office, just by owning a scale. Then do the same sort of "mock-packaging" of your item, weigh it and estimate shipping this way.

*By packaging your item rather than weighing it by itself, you are getting a much more accurate estimate. Even though it's not much, that box, bubble wrap and tape does weigh a little bit and will add to the total cost!

How to Package Your Items

Packing is one of the most important things you will do as an Ebay seller. What good is selling the item if the buyer returns it because it broke during shipping? None. This is why this is such an important step!

Make sure that the box you are packaging the item in is sturdy and can hold up to any distance of travel. The box should not be too big in relation to the item it contains. This is important in making sure that the item stays in-tact!

Once you have chosen a good, sturdy box for your item (and you can buy these in multiple sizes, for relatively little money at the post office or any office supply store or general retail store) you should make sure to wrap the item in bubble wrap or fill the box with packing peanuts.

This is important because even though you got the right size box, you still don't want it bouncing around in there at all! Remember, a broken item means a return, refund and possibly bad feedback!

Once you have the item secured safely in its packaging and the item has sold, it is time to prepare a label and send it out!

Ebay gives you a few different options for shipping labels but the most cost effective seems to be printing up the labels and shipping information through Ebay and PayPal. This way you can print out a label that already has your buyers shipping address on it. Plus, going through PayPal you can add a shipment tracker and delivery confirmation for roughly an additional $0.18. That is quite the deal for something that will prevent

18

you from the possibility of someone claiming the item was never received when it was!

Use thick, clear packaging tape to apply the label (this will also protect the label from being damaged during shipping). Also, tape up all edges to the package as this will help keep your packaging in the best condition possible.

Actions to take:

- Consider investing in a postage scale – you won't regret the amount of time this can save in the long run!

- Make sure your packaging is as good as it can be. Items that are damaged during shipping can be returned by a very unhappy customer.

- Paying a small fee for shipment tracking for you and your buyer is invaluable – never be a victim to a fraud by a customer who says they never received the order!

WHY FEEDBACK IS YOUR BIGGEST ASSET

You may not have considered one of the most influential parts of selling on Ebay and that's your feedback score. Your feedback score is determined by the number of positive and negative reviews you have gotten (neutral reviews do not affect the score). You can be reviewed both as a seller and a buyer on the same account, which can be an advantage for new sellers.

Since you are just starting out you will have no feedback score. Some people make recognize that you are just starting out and will give you a shot anyway, while others will head off to someone else's listing who has a highly positive score.

Why Feedback is So Important

Your feedback score is one of the most important things displayed on your profile. No matter how brilliantly you have composed your "About You" page, no matter how wonderful that template for your listing might be, nothing compares to a positive feedback score.

What it all comes down to is trust. Buyers will always trust sellers with positive feedback. The reason behind this is simple, would you rather go to a brand new restaurant or one that you know is good? If you want to guarantee you get the quality you want, you will go with the one you already trust.

Your feedback score will work the same way. Once you have created a positive feedback score, people will see that your products are as good as you say they are. They will trust that your "like new" condition comforter is exactly that.

Not only do you have a good chance that those buyers leaving positive reviews will become return buyers, but your new score will bring new customers in!

How to Generate Positive Feedback

Buy Items

One way for a new seller to generate a feedback score before making a sale is to purchase a couple of items (generally something you would have needed or bought anyway) through Ebay. This means the seller can rate you and you can rate them. It will help out another seller and yourself at the same time, which is awesome.

Even though people will see that you have only made purchases so far, it will still make you look like a more trustworthy candidate to buy from. Someone who is buying on Ebay is probably less likely to scam someone, after all, they wouldn't want to be scammed, right?

Communicate With Your Buyers

A buyer who feels cared for is going to leave you a much more glowing review than one who felt neglected. It works much like any other form of customer service, you make sure the customer is comfortable with the buying experience.

For example, sending out an e-mail once their payment is received is a great idea that many sellers use. This way they can let the buyer know that the order has been confirmed and will be shipped as soon as possible. Once the order is shipped, consider sending out another e-mail (with that tracking number that you paid a few extra pennies for!), this way your customer can keep track of their order until it arrives.

After the order has been delivered, give them a few days to a week to enjoy the product, but always do a follow up. Asking for feedback may feel awkward, but really, there is nothing wrong with it. Just say something simple, like this: "Hi there, I wanted to thank you again for ordering my item! If you have enjoyed the experience buying from me, I would greatly appreciate a review. I would love to leave you a positive review in return. Thank you and have a nice day!"

Make Sure Your Item Matches the Description

One big mistake that an Ebay seller can make (and that will cost them a lot in the way of negative feedback) is to not be accurate enough in your description.

For example you sell used video game controllers. They are all slightly worn and you have three of them. Make sure that if any of them have a particular problem, you state that fact. Say two are just slightly worn and it may be difficult to read the buttons, but the third one has a button that sticks.

Make sure that the buyer getting that particular controller knows that the button sticks – otherwise your "gently used" controller is likely to receive negative feedback.

In cases of electronics that are used, it may be best to offer a 30-Day-Guarantee of some sort. Either a money-back or replacement guarantee will help you avoid this kind of negative feedback – by replacing the item with a working one or a full refund, the buyer may be satisfied.

(This should only be a back-up tactic, you should always count on your buyers being happy with your items! If you wouldn't buy it in the condition it is in, don't sell it!)

Actions to take:

- Great communication is key – answer all messages promptly, ship out your items as soon as payment clears and make sure you keep in touch with your buyers. Don't be afraid to ask for positive feedback if you feel you have given them your best!

- Buy small items for personal use (or for resale but we will touch this next) and generate reviews from a buyers perspective.

BUYING ITEMS FOR RESALE: HOW IT REALLY WORKS

You will probably start to see just how lucrative selling items on Ebay can be after you sell those first initial items. After a while though you will run into a problem – you will run out of old and unused household items to sell!

Here is where it starts to get tricky. Resale is a wonderful thing and it can be very beneficial. On the other hand there is a fine line between what is considered "resale" (which will turn your casual Ebay selling into a business) and buying items, using them for a little bit and then selling them (which is not going to classify you as a business).

Depending on where you live there will be different rules that apply to owning an Ebay business that resells items. There will be taxes to pay and papers to file. This is of course, if you choose to directly resell items. Check with your local government to find out exactly what defines your sales as a business where you live before you get started!

Now assuming you are prepared to take your Ebay sales to the next level and you want to start reselling items there are a few different ways to go about it.

Garage Sales, Estate Sales and Thrift Stores

There are so many treasures to be found in garage sales and thrift stores! There are just so many things that people will throw away for a dollar or 50 cents just because they do not know it's real value! This can be a very inexpensive way to stock up on inventory for your Ebay shop and you can do it rather quickly too!

Just grab a local newspaper and check out Craigslist for all the garage sales going on over the weekend. Scout out a few that you might be interested in and go to those first. If you do not find anything of value and you still have more time you can always check out a few more! After all the chances that you visit every single sale without finding at least one deal is rare.

Estate sales are also a great way to go because often they are just trying to give the stuff away. Half of the time at an estate sale you can get top dollar items for next to nothing because all they want is to clear out the property.

Just as great of an opportunity as garage sales and estate sales is the option of going to thrift stores. These sort of stores are usually run by a charity of some kind and sell gently used items at a low cost. The best part is that these items usually have been tested prior to being put into the store to make sure it works – meaning there is a far less chance of plugging it in when you get home and finding out it doesn't work.

Discount Stores

If you are interested in selling brand name items, then one of your best assets could be to go shopping at discount stores. Retail stores like TJ Maxx, Marshalls, Ross and really any outlet store is a great place to look for a high-price designer brands at rock bottom prices.

You might be able to go through their clearance rack and find a pair of $150 jeans that they were selling for $75 and got marked down to $15 – you just have to be consistent in your searches, you will find some great things this way! (Also, you may find multiple of one item at an extremely low price. You should consider moments like these as an opportunity to stock up – buy them all and sell them at retail value!)

Buy and Sell on Ebay

Another great option is to buy items on Ebay or in local Ebay retail locations and resell them. Sometimes you will find someone who got a great deal on a whole bunch of one item and they will resell it still below market value. Whenever you find an item you know you can sell and make a profit off of, go for it! You will not only be creating a bigger inventory for yourself but you will be helping your feedback score by involving yourself in more transactions on Ebay!

Actions to take:

- Always buy in bulk when you can and you know an item will sell well.
- Learn to recognize a great deal when you see one – go to garage sales, estate sales and thrift stores to find these gems!
- Discount stores and Ebay are both places to keep an eye out for trends and great deals.

AVOID THESE COMMON NEWBIE MISTAKES

As with starting any kind of business there is a learning curb to be had. With your business on Ebay though, there are tons of sellers and successful businesses to learn from that it makes it easy to avoid some of the biggest mistakes.

Some of the biggest "newbie" mistakes that great sellers will tell you to avoid are:

Don't Over Charge for Shipping

There are many people who over estimate or over charge for shipping on their items to make up for a low starting bid. In their mind, this ensures that they will get at least close to what they think the item is worth. Luckily this practice is slowing being monitored and done away with under the new Fair Shipping rules that Ebay is implementing.

Don't Set Your Bidding or Fixed Prices Too High

When you are trying to decide what to list an item for you should avoid thinking about personal attachment to the item or what it was worth when you got it. If people find the same item at a much lower starting bid, that is where they are going to go. For items that are just cluttering up your home, isn't it worth it to get even a dollar or two, versus simply throwing the item away?

Always treat it Like a Business

From the day you start selling on Ebay you need to be thinking about your business in the long term. You may not be sure yet that you want to stick with it – but if you do you will need that 5 Star feedback from your buyers. Just think of how you would want to be treated from the buyers prospective and give them nothing less!

Get Back to Customers ASAP – Communication is KEY

If you get an e-mail about a particular item you should answer it straight away (or at least within 24 hours). This is an important part of your customer service skills in treating your Ebay selling like a business. If you want the glowing feedback and repeat customers, communication is one of the most important things you can provide. Don't think just because someone else will bid on it you shouldn't answer another's questions about an item.

Drop-Shipping is Not a Get Rich Quick Plan

For a lot of people, drop shipping looks like the best option. It gives you the opportunity to sell better items without the upfront costs. There are a couple problems with this though:

- What happens when your drop shipper is out of the item you need?

- You're buying at or near retail prices prices.

- Most of the time those drop shippers are your competition on Ebay.

Not that it never works, but drop shipping is not the great business tactic that it looks like. It is not a get rich quick scheme. If you do go with a drop shipper, stay in good communication so you know when they are out of certain items. Also make sure that you are getting the best price possible so you can still make a decent profit!

Use the Best Photo's and Descriptions Possible

Remember earlier when we said to use the best, most descriptive words you can to ensure your buyer knows exactly what they are getting? It is amazing how many people just don't do this! Tell the buyer exactly what they are getting. Use multiple photographs and make sure they are as clear as possible, showing your item from all points of view. If you don't have these things then chances are you will be passed up by your competition who is.

MAKING YOUR LIVING ON EBAY: HOW TO RUN YOUR BUSINESS

After you've gone through the process of selling your first set or two of household items you should have a good feel for how Ebay works and whether or not you want to try selling long term. If you have decided that the process is enjoyable and that you want to keep it up you have a few different routes you can choose: reselling and drop shipping are the two most common routes a seller will go.

We've already covered the basics of reselling in an earlier chapter. You can use one of many methods on how you will find the products you choose to sell (garage and estate sales, thrift stores, discount stores and even Ebay itself).

How Drop Shipping Works

With drop shipping it works a little bit differently. You list the items and once they have been paid for you use that money to purchase the item and they ship it out. It can save you time and start-up money if you still don't have a lot of it.

The only real downside is you are buying everything at or near retail costs. This means you need to either sell for slightly above or find a drop shipper who is willing to give you a good price if you can sell in high volume.

When you choose to go the drop shipping route you should be careful of how you price your items and be aware that you will probably make very little profit off of each individual item. This is not an impossible route to take, but it is more common for a successful Ebay store to be run by someone who resells items.

Ebay Stores VS Seller Account

When you start making a substantial amount of sales on Ebay it can become extremely cost effective to create an Ebay store rather than continuing to work off of a regular seller account.

There are many reasons for this but the most important to remember are:

- You get 150+ free listings.

- You can customize your web presence.

- There are tools to help you optimize and promote your store.

There are different packages ranging from $15 upwards of $180 and each as a different number of free listings per month. This is great because then you can choose the package that best fits the amount of sales that you make in the average month.

Along with the major bonus of free listings as a store owner you are provided with many other great tools. Creating a professional web presence for your store has never been easier than Ebay makes it. There are also tools that will help you to optimize not only your store but your listings as well. Plus you get tools to promote your site making it more easily found when someone searches Google, Bing or Yahoo! for the items you are selling.

On top of all that you get great discounts on things like additional photographs on your listings, lower final value fees and more. You can check out the exact tools and discounts provided with each package prior to purchase too, which helps you make the best decision for where your business currently stands in the market.

Choosing a Niche to Optimize Sales

Once you get yourself set up with a good knowledge of how selling on Ebay works, you have a decent number of positive feedback and you are preparing to set up a store many sellers will tell you it is a good idea to choose a niche.

Basically you should think about what you might like to sell long term. Try to think of things that you are knowledgeable about that would be easy to describe. For example someone who enjoys playing golf could buy and resell golf equipment.

This tactic is great because not only will it help you to narrow down the items you are looking to buy, but it also gives people a reason to remember your store. Someone that bought one really good golf club set from you and had a great customer experience is likely to come back to your store the next time they are in need of a similar product.

It also makes it easier to offer discounts on shipping by bundling as we mentioned earlier. If all your products are in a similar niche it will be easier to get people to buy multiple items from your store in one visit.

This doesn't mean that you won't still be able to sell odds and ends type items that you may find while out looking for your main product. Your store will come with the chance to separate things by categories which will make selling those odds and ends easier since they will not be jumbled in with your main niche product line.

Top Rated Seller Plus

It will take at least a year for you to reach Top Rated Seller status but it is well worth the wait! If you are planning on sticking with Ebay in the long term, this will benefit you more than even creating an Ebay store.

To become a Top Rated Seller you will need to:

- Been an active seller for 12 months or more.

- Have more than 100 transaction in that 12 months.

- Have more than $1000 in sales in that 12 months.

- You must maintain a consistent 4.8 or above for a feedback rating.

Being a Top Rated Seller will give you a Top Rated Plus badge on your Ebay listings, which will immediately tell your new customers that you are reliable and trustworthy. You will also receive a 20% discount on your final value fees and much more.

This should be something that every successful Ebay seller strives for!

Marketing

After creating your Ebay store you should consider marketing. Even though people can search through Ebay to find your items marketing will bring in a whole new crowd.

Creating a Brand

If you want to be known as a reputable seller you not only need solid feedback but you need a brand – a way for your customers to remember and recognize you. There is no way to stress how important this is if you plan on promoting your business and keeping it around long term.

A store with a catchy title is far more likely to be remembered than "Bob's Ebay Store"! Be creative, this is your business and you should make it everything you want it to be and more!

Create a memorable name for your store and create a logo of sorts to go with it. This is going to help you out a lot in the long run as it will help make sure your customers can find you again and it will help them recognize you when they see your logo around the web!

Social Media and Other Platforms for Promotion

Marketing your store is another great reason to choose a main niche area of items you want to sell. This helps to make sure that you are trying to reach one major audience rather than many individual ones.

When you are considering different ways to promote your store to any audience it is important to consider who you are trying to reach. Obviously social media is a great place to go when it comes to marketing but where else could you try? With a niche in place you can advertise on forums and blogs (as long as it's not against their Terms and Conditions) and you will be directly reaching an audience who would be interested in your products!

Back to social media for a minute though. Using platforms like Facebook and Twitter are great for advertising just about any sort of online store, whether it is through Ebay or not.

This is where your branding really starts to come into play. Every time you promote your store you should be consistent in the name of your store and the logo you use to represent it. This will help people recognize you anywhere on the web!

Old Fashion Word-of-Mouth Advertisement

No matter how advanced things may get on the World Wide Web, nothing is ever going to over shadow good ole word-of-mouth advertising!

Tell your family, friends, co-workers, tell anyone you can about your business and online store! Even if they aren't interested in the products you supply, they are bound to know somebody who is! This is completely free advertising and sometimes that is all you need to get things off the ground!

Some brick and mortar establishments still heavily rely on word-of-mouth advertising. For example Five Guy's Burgers and Fries is now famous world-wide completely from word of mouth advertising – they have never paid for a commercial on TV, the radio or internet in over 20 years!

Offer Discounts

One great tactic used by almost every business out there is to offer discounts. Whether it is a holiday sale, a clearance sale or simply a limited time offer it is still a great way to bring in new business.

Offering a product at a one-time discount for buying the first item is a great way to go about this. Once you have given them their first discounted item along with top-notch customer service they are bound to come back again and again because they trust the products you offer and your ability to take care of things on time.

YouTube

You may not want to have a TV commercial for your products, but YouTube is becoming increasingly popular. Consider using this for not only "commercials" but to build your reputation as an expert in your niche. Give tutorials on how to use certain items you sell or how to tell if one brand is better than the other for the same product.

This will not only help your reputation but it is very likely to drive your sales up! Just remember to provide a link to your Ebay store with every video you post. Also if you are using other forms of social media you can interlink all of these so that everything you post gets maximum online exposure!

Actions to take:

- Create a brand for your store.
- Use Social Media, YouTube, blogs and forums to promote your sales online.
- Tell your friends, family and anyone who will listen – they will spread the word for you!

TIPS FROM THE PROS

Use Keywords

This cannot be stressed enough – use your keywords. This is probably the best thing you can do for search optimization. The more you use certain often searched keywords the higher up your listing usually is.

Have Competitive Prices

Check out your competition and whenever possible start your auctions below the rest. This will attract buyers in large numbers, even when you are a new seller this is a great tactic.

Be Seasonal

Try to keep up with seasonal trends. It's a fact that people buy more during the holiday season and this is both true offline and online. If you have holiday themed merchandise or holiday sales you are sure to see a boost in sales for a couple months!

Always Have Good Communication

This is just as important in online customer service is in a brick and mortar retail store. Treat your customer better than you would expect to be treated. They will thank you with glowing feedback that will boost your reputation as a seller and your sales!

Make the Most of Discounts

Whenever possible you should try to allow coupons or discounts for your loyal customers. Considering sending out e-mail newsletters and promotions to your previous customers. They will appreciate it and so will your pockets!

Brand Yourself

One of the best things you can do for your business is to create a brand. Decide on an easy to remember, catchy name, design a logo (or if you aren't graphics savvy hire someone cheap at a site like Fiverr) and use it on everything. This will be how people remember you from now on and find you in the future!

Timing is everything

Be prompt with everything you do from replying to inquiries to shipping out your items. This is a big part of customer service and your buyers will appreciate your speediness. And don't forget to *communicate* with them throughout the process.

SUMMARY

After reading through this book you should be confident that you have the information and resources to get started selling on Ebay. So don't keep thinking about what could be – get going on your future now!

Even if all you do tonight is gather up those first items around the house that you are willing to part with, that is a start!

Keep it simple at first, get your feet wet. Sell those first few items, by the time you're through with those few you should know whether or not setting up shop on Ebay is right for you.

When you run out of household items start branching out, but take your time and find out what works for you! Some people can spend an entire weekend at garage sales and estate sales in search of a few rare gems, while some people may have better luck at discount stores.

Always, always, always have the best customer services! (This can never be said enough!) Be prompt, polite and you will receive loyal customers, glowing feedback and more sales!

Don't stop there, brand yourself – create a name for your business! Be proud of what you have created.

So get started – it's the only way to find out and maybe you will find that you love your Ebay business and will be one of the next Top Rated Sellers who makes their full-time living on Ebay!

Break away from the need for a 9-5 desk job and do something you love and enjoy!

OTHER BOOKS BY BRAD JONES

Fiverr Freedom: From Your First Gig To Making A Fortune On Fiverr

Blogging Brilliance: How To Make A Bundle On Your Blog

Flawless Freelance Writing: How To Make A Fortune Freelance Writing

www.ingramcontent.com/pod-product-compliance
Lightning Source LLC
Chambersburg PA
CBHW070744180526
45168CB00004B/1534